"HARE" 'N THERE
ADVENTURES OF ROSIE RABBIT
ROSIE IN EGYPT

DIANE HERAK

To order additional copies of this book, contact:
Xlibris
1-888-795-4274
www.Xlibris.com
Orders@Xlibris.com

TABLE OF CONTENTS

Diane waiting for lazy bones to get up!

We're off to the desert.

DEDICATION

This book is dedicated to my beloved family, my two Daughters, Deborah, and Amy, my six Sons, Peter, Wally, David, Mark, Dale and Christopher. To each of their spouses, or very significant other, my 17 joyous Grand-Children, and one Great Grandson, Henry.

The many children's books I've read throughout the years, and the many places I've had the pleasure of traveling, inspired me to put my thoughts and experiences in books.

I am confident that the spirits around me will guide my fingers over the keys...and will connect in my mind, so I will recall details, perhaps long forgotten, that I'd like to share.

My sister, Rosemary is important in my dedication. She is filled with surmountable strength and passion and always influenced my creativity of painting and writing. She raised me when we had no one.

Last, but surely not least my appreciation and gratitude to my soul-mate and constant companion for many years...my Jimmy K, who always supports my projects, my ideas, my life.

**In this, my second book, a very special and sincere dedication goes out to Professor Michael Stone, without whom, I would have not experienced Egypt. His knowledge, concern and supervision kept our entire group together and worry-free.*

Each day, regardless of destination or method of travel, his guidance was flawless.

III

EGYPT

Arriving at Cairo, Egypt, as our plane prepares to land,
It was a long flight...someone helped me, took my hand.

I want to see the pyramids, desert and beautiful Nile,
The hotel was near enough, so I checked in, to rest awhile.

First to Giza, the biggest pyramid, a wonder to behold,
Then a relaxing felucca ride, a type of sailboat, I was told.

The history of ancient Egypt has always been amazing to me,
Statues of Pharaohs, Kings and Queens, is what I came to see

I must ride a camel, I hope a friendly one I'll find,
The escort will lift me up, but I'm sure, he won't mind.

Open Markets, called bazaars, are busy with crowds of people,
Many magnificent mosques, all topped with a glorious steeple,

They reach up to the skies, these holy places and scream out...
"You're welcomed here in Egypt", World peace is what it's all about.

We'll pass the temple of Karnak, in Luxor, right on the Nile,
Our guide will explain its' history, the excitement makes me smile.

So I'm anxious to tell you all about my feelings, sights and things,
I will be up early tomorrow, to see what wonders the day brings.

IV

INTRODUCTION

Rosie Rabbit is about to bring you wonderful adventures about the places she travels. She will tell you of her incredible visits in many parts of the world, and also in the United States.

If you remember, in her first adventure, Rosie took us to the beautiful city of Paris, in France. She mentioned in that story that her next trip would be to Egypt. She read about the country so often and was able to watch many movies that were about Egypt, especially ancient Egypt.

While she was in Paris, she met two lovely sisters, Rosemary was from California and Diane was from Ohio. The three travelers met at several locations, and Rosie said that she wanted to make her visit to Egypt her next storybook.

Well, it was a lucky thing that Diane was there, because she knew of a very nice professor from a local college who was organizing a group to tour Egypt. She explained that it is much better to travel in a group...with a guide who was familiar with many parts of the world. Michael Stone was such a man.

Finding out that Michael had a list of about 14 interested people to make the journey seemed very exciting...so naturally, Rosie signed up. He suggested that they all meet prior to the departure date, to discuss the excursion. They did this at a restaurant, and it was very comforting that everyone was pleased that there was such a nice group. A very thorough itinerary for the 18 day venture arrived and everyone mentioned that they all better have a good camera.

Well, here is Rosie's story and wonderful pictures. Do enjoy the many places written within these pages...and as she says, "I love traveling and keeping healthy and happy. I hope everyone who reads my books will read them to their children."

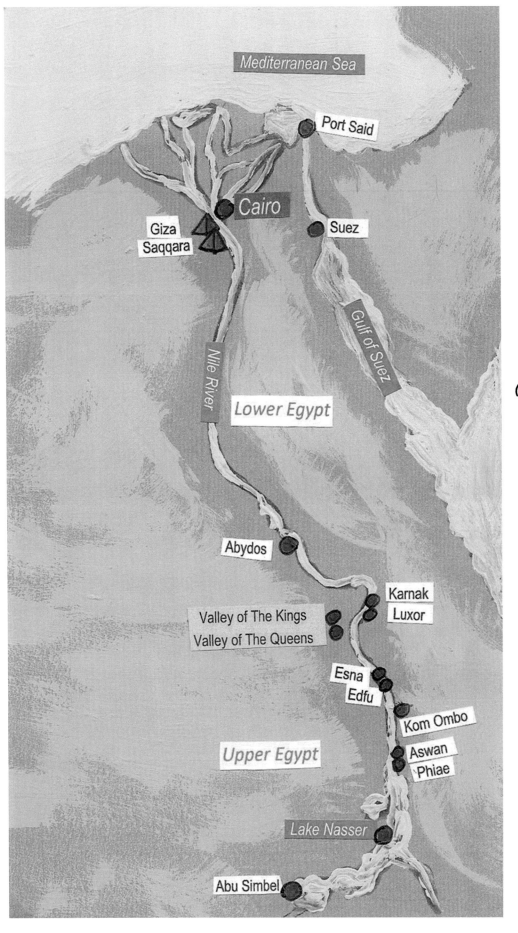

Mediterranean Sea

Port Said

Cairo

Giza
Saqqara

Suez

Gulf of Suez

Nile River

Lower Egypt

Abydos

Karnak
Luxor

Valley of The Kings
Valley of The Queens

Esna
Edfu

Kom Ombo

Upper Egypt

Aswan
Phiae

Lake Nasser

Abu Simbel

MY EGYPT MAP
OF
CITIES ON OUR TOUR

Chapter 1

CAIRO

Cairo is the capital of Egypt and the largest city in the Middle-East. In all of Africa, it is second-largest, after Lagos in Nigeria. While Lagos has a population of over 17 million, Cairo has 6 million but 10 million live just outside of the city, considered Greater Cairo. These figures were printed in brochures that I picked up to read.

There are over 4 million cars in this fascinating city, and I think I saw most of them. When so many cars were not stopping at street lights, or not having the car lights on, the driver said that stop signs, street lights or car lights are optional. In other words, there is no law that says a driver needs to obey the rules. That was unreal and I felt I would be involved in an accident every time I got into an automobile.

One of the oldest universities in the world is in Cairo. It is the al-Azhar, founded in 970-972 as a center for learning. Formal education is very important in Cairo. A formal education, the guide explained, means 12 years of schooling, and although public schools are free, the school system has been under-funded for years. However, many families can afford to send their children to private schools. At the end of the 12 years, the children take an exam similar to the SAT in The U.S., and then their exams determine what is available for the students in order to continue their education.

Cairo, as other large cities, has problems with high levels of pollution and traffic. Their metro is one of two on the continent of Africa and among the fifteenth busiest in the world. Our guide told us that over 500 million people ride the metro every year, and 12 million tons of goods are transported on the metro.

There are over a dozen wonderful hotels to stay in when visiting Cairo. Many are within walking distance of the Giza Pyramids, some along the Nile, and others just minutes from museums and wonderful attractions.

I found a very helpful guide who agreed to take me to the Cairo Museum. This lovely huge pink building is a History museum that has a collection over 100,000 items, covering 5,000 years from ancient Egypt. Much of the collections are kept in storerooms. It was established in 1902. I was excited to see the King Tutankhamen treasures, along with the solid Gold Mask that he was buried with. King Tutankhamen was known as the "Boy King" because he took the throne of King at the age of 9. He ruled for about 10 years and died of an unknown reasons when 19 years old. Many books have been written about King Tut (as he was called), but no one ever seem to really know the truth about how he lost his life.

A British archaeologist, Howard Carter worked for years in an area of Egypt called, "The Valley of the Kings." We were told that in 1922 (some said the year was 1923), he discovered the tomb of this young King, and it was an unbelievable find for the whole world. This valley was chosen for Pharaohs and powerful nobles' graves. Over 60 tombs were found there, according to information we were told.

Of seven "Ancient Wonders of the World", The only remaining one is in Cairo...that is the Great Pyramid of Giza.

The Cairo Museum

A view from the bus

3

Elegant shopping in Egypt. Few items we purchased.

Chapter 2

PYRAMIDS

There are about 100 pyramids in Egypt, the first, we are told, was built over 4,000 years ago in a burial ground called Saqqara. This area is near the Egyptian city of Memphis. North of Saqqara is Abusir, and South is Dahshur. The space from Giza, known for the many ancient monuments, to Dahshur was used as a cemetery by people who lived in Memphis in ancient times. Dahshur is located on the West Bank of the Nile River, about 25 miles South of Cairo. This entire area was named as a "World Heritage Site" by UNESCO, which stands for *"United Nations Educational, Scientific and Cultural Organization."* This organization catalogues names and conserves sites of outstanding cultural or natural importance to humanity. How very nice to have such foundations to protect the past.

This first pyramid was called a step pyramid. Our guide tells us that when it was built it had a flat top, built over 2600 years B.C. After some time, "steps" were added on top and it then had 6 steps. It was almost 200 feet tall and the burial chambers that were for the Pharaoh and the royal families were underneath the ground, hidden by tunnels. After that 16 Egyptian kings built similar ones in this area. Many are falling apart and constantly being worked on to preserve them.

The Great Pyramid of Giza is one of three and the largest. Another name for this Ancient Wonder is the Pyramid of Khufu. Just as those built in Saqqara, these were constructed for Pharaoh and their families. After they passed away, the bodies were mummified and placed in the many chambers and passages. This Great Pyramid was the tallest building made by man for over 3500 years. When built, it was 483 feet tall. Because of erosion, the height now measures 456 feet.

The Egyptian Pharaoh Khufu, was why the Great Pyramid of Giza was built. It took about 20 years to construct this pyramid that had three burial chambers. One of the chambers was said to have been built in the rock under the pyramid. The King's chamber was the highest, while the Queen's was just above ground. History says that Khufu did not mean for any of his wives to be buried in the chamber, but used it for a statue of himself.

In the building of this pyramid, there are more than 2 million stone blocks that weighed almost 6 million tons. It is the only one in Egypt that has entrances that go up and go down. The king's chamber was closed to visitors, but I was glad about that because we were warned that one has to walk all the way down, bent over. I thought, hmmmm, was that ordered to be built like that so that visitors would have to bend, or bow down to honor what the chamber represented? But maybe not.

The cement, sand or water that was used to build the pyramid, we were told, cannot be made today. It is unknown how they mixed the mortar that holds the blocks together so tightly and perfectly that one cannot even slip a thin razor in- between the enormous blocks. The stone that was used is not as strong as the cement or filling that holds together all of these blocks. There have been documentaries showing experienced engineers and builders attempting to duplicate an Egyptian pyramid, just as many books explain how they were built. It was not possible to do.

I saw one of the sisters that I met in Paris. Diane from Ohio was going into the largest pyramid and allowed me to take a picture of her coming down the steep steps. Her sister, Rosemary could not make the trip. We agreed to meet while touring Egypt.

Anyone can see photographs, or watch videos about these great wonders, but to see them in person is something that cannot be described or imagined…these Egyptian pyramids from another lifetime…another era.

Amazing pyramid sights

climbing down from the largest
pyramid of Giza

Looking up

Chapter 3

THE SPHINX

The colossal statue of the Sphinx is a mythological, or imaginary beast-like creature with the body of a lion and the head of a person. The head, information tells us, was supposed to be of a Pharaoh or an Egyptian God. It goes on to say that as different Pharaohs ruled Egypt, they wanted the face of the sphinx to resemble them.

The Great Sphinx of Giza, is one of the largest statues in the world… and certainly the oldest. Our guide informs us that archeologists say it was carved somewhere around 2500 BC. They go on to tell us that the head was carved to look like Pharaoh Khafra. This magnificent Sphinx faces the sunrise and it appears to guard the pyramid tombs of the Giza Plateau.

This Great Sphinx was carved out of bedrock in a trench right at the Giza site. It is a huge figure, 241 feet long, 20 feet wide and 66 feet high. The eyes are 6 feet tall and the ears about 3 feet wide. When built, the nose, we are told, would have been 5 feet long, however it was broken off, no idea when.

Weather and erosion of the sand wore away much of the statue over the past 4500 years, and it would have looked much different. It had a long-braided beard and a nose. Archeologists determine that it was painted bright colors, such as the body was painted red, the beard, blue and the headdress most probably was yellow.

In a city named Thebes, within a modern city called Luxor, is a long boulevard lined with sphinxes. Quite a sight to see, and all looking alike, so powerful and regal, sitting with pride for actually thousands of years. They still hold their position…they still await the many millions of visitors who are amazed and so pleased that they made the journey to call on them.

There is very interesting legend that has been written about, and the Egyptians will tell you the story about the Prince and Great Sphinx of Giza. This is my favorite story while visiting Egypt.

"Thutmose IV was a Prince in Egypt, son of Pharaoh Amenhotep. The young prince had many brothers and half-brothers who always told lies about him because they knew he was the Pharaohs favorite to succeed him. They said the Prince was not worthy of someday being Pharaoh. One day there was a great festival a few miles down the Nile River. The Prince wanted to get away from all the celebrations to go into the desert. He took 2 of his servants with him, and they stopped to rest under some palm trees. But he wanted to be alone, so he drove his chariot away saying good-bye and told them to wait and he would return. The trip took him to Giza and to the three man-made mountains of stone…the Pyramids. Many long centuries had passed after Khafra was placed to rest in the pyramid. The sands of the desert had blown against the Great Sphinx, until it was totally covered except for his head and shoulders, and a small ridge in the sand where its back was.

The Prince decided to take a nap right in front of the great rock carving. While he slept, he dreamed that the Sphinx moved a little, struggling and trying to get out of the sand. He then whispered to the Prince, saying he was smothering and vowed he would become Pharaoh, if would he remove the sand that was surrounding him. Thutmose did promise, and said he would build a shrine to the Sphinx. Then the two servants, who were searching for him, found the Prince and the three of them rode back to his home. Soon after, the Pharaoh Amenhotep announced that his son, Thutmose would be heir to the throne."

He did become King of Egypt, and one of her greatest Kings.

An Egyptian mythology site posted this.

"Just a hundred and fifty years ago- 3,230 years after Thutmose IV became Pharaoh of Egypt- the Sphinx, again buried to the neck in sand, was dug out by an early archaeologist. Between its paws he found the remains of a shrine in which stood a red granite tablet, fourteen feet high. Inscribed on it in hieroglyphs was the whole story of the Prince and the Sphinx. The tablet also tells us that it was set there in fulfillment of his vow to Pharaoh Thutmose IV in the third month of the first year of his reign, after he cleared away all the sand which hid him from sight. Harmachis, the Great Sphinx that had been made in the days of Khafra, when the world was young."

Now isn't that a wonderful story? I guess there was "bullying" even thousands of years ago…how sad, but it proves that the one who always wins is the one getting the harassment, one way or another.

Amazing Egyptian sights.

A method of travel for us

Two lonely monuments from the Ramesside period.

Ramses II is wearing
the double crown of
Lower and Upper
Egypt as a symbol for
the united country

Chapter 4

THE FELUCCA RIDE

Next on my agenda was to enjoy a "felucca" sail on the Nile. The Nile River has always been so interesting to read about. Now here I was, not only looking at it, but knowing I would be sailing on it. Before my vacation here is over, we will be on a cruise ship...on the Nile! I am going to try to go on the cruise with Diane. She will love it, I'm certain. But more about that in the last chapter.

We had a choice of taking the 2-hour felucca sail in the daytime, or the evening. There were nice reasons to select either. The daytime would give us the warm sunshine and breezes as we sailed. Also, sights of the shoreline, and the sounds of those who lived near the river, tending their animals or playing with the children would be an experience to remember. However, a night sail would allow us to see the sunset and hear the songs of many who would serenade the felucca tourists. I wanted to see the shoreline and so I chose a day sail.

A felucca is a sailboat, made partially of wood. There are no engines or motorized boats in this line. We are told that feluccas have changed very little over the years, and it is dependent totally on the breezes of Egypt. Our guide also told us that in Egypt, there is always a southerly wind that pushes the feluccas up the Nile River. Then on the return it sails nicely on the current going downstream.

We were introduced to about 10 passengers, like me, who are first timers to tour the Nile, and to enjoy a felucca ride. Then we met the two experienced people to handle the duties of the boat, and one of our guides to accompany us on this exciting and thrilling sail on this famous river.

Our guide explained that for centuries, the felucca was the only way that those in Egypt could get around to the different areas, and so much freight and baggage was shipped on a felucca. All of us on the trip agreed that it was really nice that the tradition of this type of sail continued even after the ancient Egypt times.

So we were on our way...a soft breeze and warm sunshine made the time even nicer than we thought. The man, who I thought was probably the "captain" of the boat, tied the apparel that he was wearing around his waist, and steered with his feet. He smiled and pointed to his feet, knowing we would all be surprised at his talent. After a short time, I spotted several oxen, in the water, being sort of "bathed" by their owners. The family waved to us and sent happy sounds to our group. It was sort of surprising to see the coast line so close on each side. The greenery on the shores was amazing in fullness and color. I thought that probably whatever crops Egyptians grow must do very well in gardens on the banks of the Nile.

Children were playing in the water everywhere as we journeyed along and the "crew" offered bottles of water and pastries. I wondered if he carried any carrots or lettuce, no I was told, so I gave one of the treats a try. Very good! Perhaps I could get used to this type of delicacy. Many of these felucca tours are very long, often several days, but the several hours that ours was scheduled was just fine for me.

The trip was over and our patient guide seemed pleased that we all were enjoying the wonderful tour on this sailboat called a felucca.

Egyptian sights from our boat, and the tour bus.

Chapter 5
FLOWERS & DESERT PLANTS

Flowers grow beautifully along the banks of the Nile. In ancient times, it is written that Egypt was the first country identified as having a national flower. Both the Lotus and Papyrus represented Upper and Lower Egypt. The White lotus, also known as the Water Lily grows nicely in water or very damp soil. A flower shop owner explained that the Lily could be white or blue. The blue flower has more pointed petals, with smooth leaves, while the white lily has rounded petals and their leaves are not smooth.

Papyrus is the other plant well known as Egypt's symbol. This plant grows very tall, well over 10 feet, we are told. The stem of the papyrus had many uses in ancient times, as well as modern. These strong stalks made good chairs, boats and other household items. The leaves were peeled and made into strips, then pressed together for many days. The fluid from the tightly pressed strips would sort of "glue" together and after hammering and drying in the sun. The sheets were used for writing or painting. Egypt's bazaars and small shops are filled with beautiful paintings on papyrus sheets.

Papyrus in Egypt was grown and used for thousands of years. Today other tree and plant sources are used to make paper, however, for the tourists, papyrus is still popular.

Other flowers grown in Egypt are Thistle, Jasmine, Chrysanthemum, Iris, Corn Flower and the little Marjoram bush, to name a few. It has been well documented that Queen Cleopatra, and many other Queens of Egypt, used powder made from Flower petals, rocks and minerals for eye makeup. An Egyptian historian told us that the eye makeup also protected the women from the intense rays of the sun.

While visiting a small but very busy perfume shop, the flowers of Egypt was being discussed. The workers said that flowers from Egypt are exported to Paris for use in the most expensive perfumes that Paris manufactures.

We are told that Egypt ships hundreds of tons of flowers to other countries in the world, primarily to Europe.

The Sahara Desert is said to be the largest in the world. The temperature during the day is well over 120 F, but usually falls below freezing during the night. Only a few inches of rain falls in this desert every year, however there are many hundreds of types of plants that grow and are accustomed to this kind of difficult climate.

A tree called the Date Palm has been a part of the desert in the Nile Valley for thousands of years, growing almost 80 feet tall. These trees can live and provide wonderful dates for over 100 years.

The fig tree is also a very important "bush" can grows to about 25 feet tall. People living in the area depend on the wonderful fruit that is produced by this tree. It is said that in Africa, there are over 100 types of fig trees.

Another important plant that grows nicely in Egypt is the Olive Tree. It is an evergreen that will grow up to 35 feet and survives the heat of the desert for hundreds of years. Olive Oil is excellent for the heart and is used by many people in the world.

Flowers, Papyrus & Olive Trees.

Chapter 6
RUGS & CARPETS

A lovely carpet company was next on the agenda. I think I expected to see carpets that resemble a style of Oriental Rugs. But they did not look that type at all. The people in charge of the establishment were very kind and anxious to show us around.

There were rugs and carpets hanging from the ceiling in several rooms of the display areas. The one that I purchased was extremely inexpensive and woven by a girl who told us she was 13 years of age. These rugs were not manufactured with high tech machinery, but instead with vertical looms that she wove with sticks, such as rods, and her bare feet. The measurements were 24"x40" and the design was amazing...green background with 4 palm trees and a sun at the top. What appeared as a stone home or building, next to the 3 pyramids of Giza. What was really surprising was that the other side of this tight-weaved wool carpet was the identical design. As she did the weaving, it produced a two-sided scene. Along the bottom, in the center reflections of the sun, or perhaps the moon nearing evening. Of course the rug is not used as a floor cover, but it is hanging on the wall as a mural.

Many rugs and carpets made in Egypt are considered among the best in the world.

Carvings of rug makers and their looms can be found in many tombs and museums. This method of carpet making, we're told, dates back 2000 B.C.

Carpets and fabric from a local market (Bazaar.)

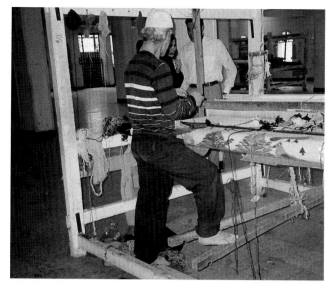

Chapter 7

THE GODDESS SELKET

I mentioned a little about the amazing Cairo Museum, but I would like to tell you of my very favorite Egyptian Goddess, whose name is Selket. Now there are several different spellings of her name, however, I am going by what I was told at the museum, and what I read in the story of King Tutankhamun.

Beautiful Selket is one of 4 goddesses that protect the King's organs. The organs are preserved in four carved alabaster stoppers for the miniature coffins which hold King Tut's organs. His heart remained in the body. The alabaster chest is a type of a white stone, that was then placed in a large gold canopic chest. The size of this outer gold chest is 79" high, 49" wide, and the depth is 60".

Outside, along each of the four walls, stands a goddess. Beautiful Selket has her arms tenderly outstretched and her head is turned a little to protect the treasure she was chosen for. She is made of gold with a delicate looking garment, head-dress and serious yet glorious eye makeup. On her head sits a scorpion, ready to attack should she give the order. She is said to protect those who worship her by healing snake bites, stings and any poisonous bite.

I did ask how tall the statue of Selket was, but I do not know for certain. Looking at the outer gold chest that is said to be almost 80"...she looks to be around 3 to 4 feet tall. Not sure, but it is fun to guess.

ENTRANCE TICKETS TO A FEW OF OUR SCHEDULED TOURS

Mit - Rahina — 14 L.E.

Citadel of Salah al-Din — 20 L.E.

The Egyptian Museum — 20 L.E.

The Royal Mummies Hall (The Egyptian Museum) — 40 L.E.

Kom-Ombo Temple

THE VALLEY OF THE KINGS (three tombs) — 20 LE — 230124

TOMB OF MERENPTAH

THE FOUR KING OF THE ,,TH DYNASTY THIS TOMB IS CONSIDERED ONE OF THE GREATEST TOMBS AND IS DISTINGUISHED WITH ITS BEAUTIFAL REMA_INING INSCRIPTIONS THE TEXTS OF RÉ PRAYERS BOOK GATES BOOK AND WHAT IS EXISTS IN THE NETHERWORLD.

- ENTRANCE
- FIRS CHAMBER
- BURIAL CHAMBER

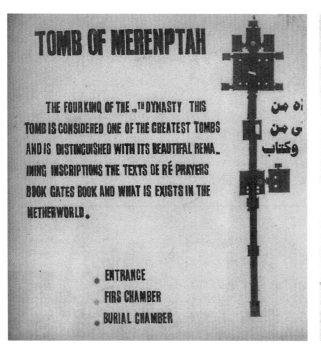

SACRED LAKE

ALL THE ANCIENT EGYPTIAN TEMPLE HAD A SACRED LAKE FOR PURIFICATION IT SYMBOLIZES TO THE PRIMORDIAL OCEAN AT THE BEGINNING OF CREATION. AMUN'S SACRED LAKE'S AREA IS ABOUT 80 X 40 M .IT WAS PROBABLY CONSTRUCTED BY THOTMOSIS III SURROUNDED BY A HUGE WALL CONNECTED TO THE SEVENTH PYLON AT THE NORTHWESTERN CORNER THERE IS A COLOSSAL SCARAB IS MADE OF ROSE GRANITE.

YORK WELCOME YOU TO LUXOR

Akhnaton and his family offering to Aton

The golden Mask of King Tut Ankh Amun 18th Dyn.

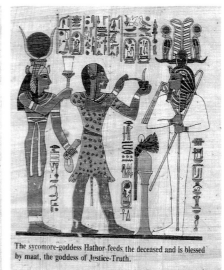

The sycomore-goddess Hathor feeds the deceased and is blessed by maat, the goddess of Justice-Truth.

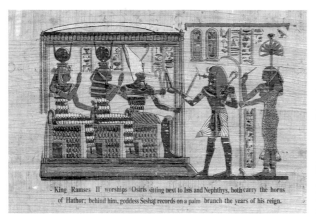

- King Ramses II worships Osiris sitting next to Isis and Nephthys, both carry the horns of Hathor; behind him, goddess Seshat records on a palm branch the years of his reign.

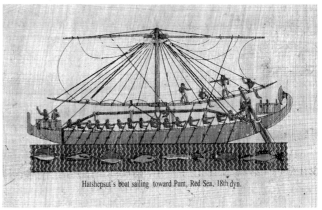

Hatshepsut's boat sailing toward Punt, Red Sea, 18th dyn.

Chapter 8

THE NILE RIVER

The Nile River is the longest river in the world. It is about 4,160 miles. That means if you look at a map of The United States...depending where you think the furthest points are, it is about 3,000 miles from coast to coast. So, The Nile River is over one thousand miles longer that it is from our West coast to the East coast. That is a very long river.

It is totally located in Africa, but runs along 10 different countries. In Northern Egypt is where the Nile drains into the Mediterranean Sea. That area is known as the Nile Delta. Because of the rich soil due to the Nile, the farming has been wonderful for thousands of years. Half of Egypt's population live in this Nile Delta area. That is about 40 million people.

Before 1970, flooding of the Nile ruined crops and then years of the levels of the river being very low, made the area experience drought and famine for the crops and the animals. Then The Aswan High Dam was built and that totally controlled the water levels. I will write more about that after a few more chapters. The Nile would flood every year near the end of summer and into September. In the Ethiopian Mountains, melting snow along with much rain flowed down into the Nile, causing flooding. When I told you about our Felucca ride, our boat passed many temples where you could see the stains on the temple where, when the flooding took place and almost destroyed the ancient temples. I will explain about the re-locating of some of the temples and monuments.

For thousands of years, clay from the delta was used for pottery making. The area was also excellent for fishing. Some of the fish that could be found there were catfish, Nile perch, eels, tilapia and many more. Hippopotamuses and crocodiles lived in the swamp areas.

Another very important event that was associated with the Nile Delta was the finding of the Rosetta Stone. French soldiers that were rebuilding a fort in Egypt near the Mediterranean Sea, found this amazing stone, in a small village called Rosetta. The slab of stone was said to be carved around 196 B.C. It was very large and weighed over a thousand pounds.

For centuries, Egyptian hieroglyphics could not be interpreted by anyone. It was not until the 1820's that a French man was able to translate the message on the stone. There were three different writings, all saying the same thing, The first carved writing was in hieroglyphic, the second in demotic (a well-known script in Egypt), and the third in Greek. It was said to have been written by priests saying good things that a King of Egypt did for them and the people of Egypt.

This discovery opened up an entirely new way for scholars and well-educated people to read and understand the multitude of hieroglyphic writings in tombs and the walls of temples in Egypt. So the message on the stone was not really that important, many say, but understanding the languages was a treasure in itself.

View of the Nile & Rosettsa Stone.

Chapter 9

LUXOR / KARNAK

Luxor, once known as Thebes, has been referred to as an "open air museum on both sides of the Nile." The town side, which is on the east, is where one can find the Temple of Luxor, and the Temple of Amon-Ra at Karnak. The Western side is the Valley of the Kings, Valley of the Queens along with hundreds of tombs and grand mortuary temples. Egyptians often call Luxor a "village", but has a population of over 100,000 and an international airport where as many as 2,000 tourists arrive each day. Aswan, on the other hand has twice the population and thriving commerce, but without international flights.

From the river, Luxor is almost hidden due to all of the cruise ships and various boats all tied up, often 4 or 5 deep along the two or three miles of the eastern bank. There are always several ferry boats, crossing to the western bank.

Karnak, which is located between the ancient cities of Luxor and Thebes is said to be one of the most magnificent temple complexes ever built. In Karnak are huge pillars, avenues of sphinxes, unbelievable towers, an exceptional obelisk that is 97 feet tall and weighs over 300 tons. There is the "Great Hypostyle Hall", one of the largest single chambers that has ever been built. It covers nearly 54,000 square feet. They say that the Cathedral of Notre Dame in Paris, could comfortably fit within the walls of this amazing hall.

In Luxor/Karnak and many locations on the way.

Pillars, Archeologists, Queen Hatshepsut's Temple.

More sights of Egypt...Temples, Tombs.

Diane, passing out lipstick, candy, pencils and tablets
to the local women and children.

Pretending to cut stone, posing in front of a temple,
and with our tour organizer, Michael Stone.

DEIR EL BAHARY FACTORY
FOR ALABASTER & HAND MADE
مصنع الدير البحري للالباستر والشغل اليدوي

تمثال أبو الهول المرمري
ALABASTER SPHINX
→

SITE OF MEMPHIS
RAMSSES II MUSEUM
THE TEMPLE OF PTAH
THE TEMPLE OF APIS
THE TEMPLE OF HATHOR
THE TEMPLE OF RAMSSES

مقبرة بتاح حتب
اسرة خامسة ٢٤٠٠ ق.م
TOMB OF PTAH-HOTEP
DYN V
C. 2400 B.C.

Tomb of
Nefertari →

TELESTAR TRAVEL
M//S LADY SARA
TELESTAR 1
CAIRO 1-TAHRIR SQUARE TEL.: 3544600/3556491
FAX 3562670 TIX 22652 LUXOR 580450 ASWAN 326956/323092

TOMB OF
TUT ANKH AMON
NO. 62

31

Chapter 10

ABU SIMBEL & UNFINISHED OBELISK

The Abu Simbel temples are two huge rock temples in Abu Simbel, in Nubia, Southern Egypt. Lake Nasser is where the temples are located, on the western bank about 142 miles from Aswan. These twin temples were carved in the 13th century BC, from the mountainside. The entire structure was re-located in 1968 due to threats of flooding and avoiding being totally covered in water during the reservoir of Lake Nasser that formed after the building of the Aswan High Dam.

This magnificent structure took about 20 years to be completed, and was one of six rock temples built in Nubia during Ramesses II long reign. The purpose, we learn, was to express ego and much pride in the great Pharaoh.

The unfinished obelisk is the largest ancient obelisk known. It is located in the northern area of ancient Egypt, in Aswan, at the stone quarries.

When cracks appeared during its construction, the project was abandoned. If this structure would have been completed, it would have been the heaviest obelisk that was ever carved in ancient Egypt.

The obelisk would have been about 140 feet in length and weighed almost 1100 tons. It is still attached to the bedrock. Being that the construction of the obelisk was most probably during the reign of Queen Hatshepsut, it is believed that she ordered it to celebrate her 16th year in power. This, larger than any other, would have been similar to her obelisk that is in the Karnak Temple in Luxor.

A fascinating place to visit is this Northern Quarry for those who would like to see the early technologies of the Egyptian worker, and designer. Much has been learned from this monument that came to an end, as far as the techniques in stone-cutting and use of tools.

It was very nice to be able to get so very close to this amazing rock formation that was abandoned. There are wooden walkways and platforms to view the obelisk quite closely. I took many pictures of this absolutely ancient historic would-be obelisk.

Obelisks and unfinished stone from thousands of years ago.

Always digging for answers to the past. Hieroglyphics tell a story.

Chapter 11

ASWAN HIGH DAM

As we rode along for hours in a very comfortable bus, in the distance I spotted a massive monument of some sort that looked like 5 spires reaching up into the sky. Our guide informed us that this was the Aswan High Dam. What a really beautiful and modern structure this monument represented.

Our guide explained that an Aswan Low Dam was constructed between 1898-1902, across the Nile. Now this new 20th century engineering achievement was said to be one of the largest in the world. The purpose of the dam was to protect Egypt from the high Nile floods sending large sections of the land into the Mediterranean. With this new dam, it would be large enough to stop the flooding and electric power could benefit more than half the overall supply power supply that Egypt uses.

Because of the building of this new High Dam, many ancient Egyptian monuments had to be moved out of the way so that the floods would not ruin them. A huge water supply, called a reservoir was formed because of this dam, it was named Lake Nasser. This lake was 300 miles long and almost 10 miles wide. Many thousands of people of Egypt had to be moved to different areas to find somewhere else to live. The construction of this High Dam was very expensive and took 10 years to complete. It was finished in 1970.

More than 50 million cubic yards of earth and rock were needed to build the dam. This meant there was more than 15 times more rock used than was in the Great Pyramid at Giza. That is pretty hard to imagine... but it is a true fact about this amazing Aswan High Dam.

Aswan High Dam.

Chapter 12

A CRUISE ON THE NILE

The last 4 days and 3 nights of my unbelievable trip to Egypt was spent on a lovely cruise ship called The Nile Goddess. It was very comfortable and accommodating and the crew and staff just could not have done more for out group. The buffets that were served and rooms were wonderful. During the day, we enjoyed the deck as we delighted in the beautiful Nile, and the majestic rays of the sun. Then in the evenings, the cruise line had very nice events to keep us happy and excited to see what was planned.

Diane had so much fun dancing in the evenings with other passengers and the beautifully costumed Egyptians. Before she left Ohio, she purchased a set of castanets…but they were not wooden, they were metal. She danced for hours and the rest of our group danced right along with the wonderful music.

We stopped each day to visit the astonishing sights of ancient Egypt, that I wrote about in the former chapters. Instead of explaining our trip in order, I wanted to end the book with the Nile cruise. We passed unforgettable sights on the banks of the Nile, and saw other cruise ships with happy tourists, waving to us and calling out greetings.

There was posted around the ship an announcement of invitation to a "Galabia Party". The cruise line had many costumes to select from and we all had fun deciding which we should wear. There was a buffet of amazing foods, beverages and of course fun and music. Native dancers were on hand to instruct us as to the very interesting steps of the dances. They seemed to appreciate our enthusiasm as we did theirs.

It was very difficult to accept the fact that this wonderful tour of Egypt was nearing the end. None of us were very "bubbly" on that last day, instead we were all talking about the beauty and the delight of having the privilege of making such a trip. Many of us agreed that we were thrilled as to the many pictures we took and informative brochures that were offered to us. We did not want to ever forget all that we saw and experienced.

Diane said that she had enough to make at least 5 huge scrapbook/pictures albums, which she did. I found her on the deck looking out at the moon and the dark sky. The day had come to an end, but not ever to be forgotten. She said she was inspired to write a poem about Egypt and her actually seeing so much what was ancient Egypt...the temples, pyramids and what life may have been like.

As for me, it was an experience of a lifetime...another wonderful adventure to write about for my dear friends and readers. I left Egypt... anxious to return home and put it in writing. Then wondering where I shall plan to vacation next? One thing crossed my mind, this will be a pretty hard act to follow...this country, this beautiful place in the world... called Egypt.

The cruise lobby and sun deck.

The cruise dining area and beautiful buffet.

Our fearless leader, Michael Stone getting some rays.

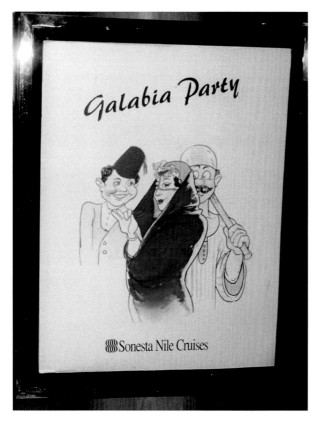

AUTHOR'S NOTE

The time that I spent in Egypt, will be forever in my mind, as an amazing awareness of how life must have been thousands of years ago. It is equally satisfying to know of the hundreds of thousands of tourists that look forward to the sights of Egypt by enjoying the information that the guides tirelessly explain at each and every area that is included on the journey.

Spending the final days of our tour, on a cruise ship on the Nile, left all of us rather somber and slowly going through the routine of the day. All I could think about was that when I returned home, I was going to immediately write a poem about the experience, a once-in-a-lifetime adventure that I was fortunate to have been a part of. That poem is printed in its entirety on the last page of this book.

The photograph below is one that I took just before the brilliant Egyptian sun replaced the tranquil night sky. It seems that nothing could be seen...but that is why I took it. The effect tells it all. Also, the picture is of me, moments before we arrived back at our destination port. Just me and the Nile...that was all.

Adieu Beloved Nile

Farewell, Dearest Nile...my benevolent friend
And to Egypt, your sights now come to an end.

I've seen night turn to day, on your timeless shore
Never resisting the change, somehow expecting much more
Of your memorable past, the struggle and pain
From temples and tombs, still does remain

The glory of life, as you knew all too well
Unlike any on earth, the ancients will tell

Of the wonder of those, Egypt called its' own
Wrapped in linens and oils, gently draping skin and bone

Rest well, dear brothers and sisters of the sand
Angels have come to take you by the hand
For death does not exist, as many have been taught
Fate seemed unfair, wars had to be fought

But a new day is dawning, and glory at last,
Far below your majestic Sphinx, are answers to the past

And present and future, together be revealed
All that's been hidden, forgotten and sealed
As King, Queen and Pharaoh, Commoner or such,
Resume places in Egypt, every heart will they touch

But you my patient Nile, winding on, as shores are kissed
Perhaps you understand so well, how greatly you'll be missed

Your picture, I gaze at, with joy and a tear
I'll behold you again...another time, another year.

Diane Herak

Printed in the United States
By Bookmasters